BOOK I

By: J. Allen

Illustrations by:

Dreamtime.com

vecteezy.com

J. Allen

The Adventures of Earl the Human Pearl and Friends

By: J. Allen

Illustrations by: www.dreamtime.com, ClipartOf.com, vecteezy.com, Rock Patterson, and J. Allen

Cover Illustrated by: Dreamtime.com

Cover created: Jazzy Kitty Publishing

Logo designs by: Andre M. Saunders and Leroy Grayson

Editor(s): Jacqueline Allen and Anelda L. Attaway

©2014 Jacqueline Allen

ISBN: 978-0-9916648-6-3

Library of Congress Control Number: 2014958998

All rights reserved. This book is protected under the copyright laws of the United States of America. This book may not be copied or reprinted for commercial gain or profit. This Book is a work of fiction. All characters and events portrayed in this book are either products of the author's imagination and are used fictionally. The use of short quotations or occasional page copying for personal or group study is permitted and encouraged. Permission will be granted upon request. For Worldwide Distribution. Printed in the United States of America. Published by Jazzy Kitty Greetings Marketing & Publishing, LLC dba Jazzy Kitty Publishing. Utilizing Microsoft Publishing Software.

DEDICATIONS

This Book is dedicated to my niece Jackie, my Family Members and my Co-Workers who encouraged me to keep writing and finish the Story of Earl and to all those who still loves Super Heroes no matter how old they are.

TABLE OF CONTENTS

Book 1 – Introduces and tells the Story of Earl and his four Friends i
The Beginning – The Story of Earl 01
Chapter 2 – The Rescue 09
Chapter 3 – The Story of Nix 14
Chapter 4 – The Story of Merlo 22
Chapter 5 – The Story Malia and Celia 26
Chapter 6 – The Quest to Find Earl 30
Chapter 7 – Ultimus Maximus versus the Tasers 37
Chapter 8 – Maci Twins are Kidnapped 44
Chapter 9 – Earl is Ambushed in Korea 50
Book 2 – The Search for Earl's Mother 54
About the Author 57

BOOK 1

Introduces and tells the Story of Earl and his four Friends

Earl is a young man who will discover he is destined to become someone special. From time to time, he is haunted by bad dreams that he does not understand. Earl has a little Birthmark on his arm that he does not like.

Earl will later discover that this little Birthmark holds the key to his destiny that is hiding deep inside of him. One day he will meet a young Man with Supernatural abilities who will reveal to him what he is destined to become.

Along the way, he will meet three more Friends with extraordinary abilities. Earl and the others will become very close Friends. They will learn Martial Arts and will become the Masters of it.

Along the way, the five friends will discover that when they are combined together as a group they can be an unstoppable force. They will call this force the Ultimus Maximus. Just like any other Heroes, there has to be a Villain or Villains. The Ultimus Maximus will be forced to reveal themselves on one particular Stormy Day and this will change their destinies forever.

Five hundred years ago a small Meteorite made its way across the Universe with Earth in its path

After some time, the Meteorite made its way through Earth's Atmosphere and slammed into the Ocean and sank to the bottom.

It remain there unnoticed and undiscovered for five hundred years until now. 25 Years later

Earl's Story begins.

THE BEGINNING

The Story of Earl

The Smith Family who names are Diamond the Father, Crystal the Mother, Amber and Jasper the Children were packing and getting ready for their Summer Vacation. Everyone was so excited to finally have some fun and to take a break from the chill of the winter. They packed up the Car and drove to the Coast of Florida to the Family's favorite vacation spot on the Beach and near Crystal's childhood home. They arrived around 3:00 p.m. They unpack their luggage and Crystal prepared everyone Dinner. Crystal mentioned, "I hope we get a chance to see the Meteor Shower tonight." After Dinner Diamond said, "Let's go out and watch the Meteor shower." The Meteor shower came and went and they all went to bed for the night.

The next day the Family decided to take their new Boat out to go fishing. So the Family loaded up their Boat with food and fishing supplies and took off to go catch some fish. While the Family was out fishing, Diamond notices some strange, unusual looking clouds coming toward them. He thought, *"Those are some strange looking clouds,"* but he continues to fish. Crystal went below deck to prepare some snacks for the Family. As she was preparing the snacks, she notices that the Boat was starting to sway back and forth. She became nervous and went back up above deck. Crystal said, "Diamond what is happening?" Diamond answered and said, "I don't know." He said, "It started to rain a little then all of a sudden it was a downpour." The storm formed so fast and quickly there was not time to react, not even time to go below deck to retrieve and put on their life jackets.

Then the Family heard a loud crackling sound. They all looked around and saw that a lightning bolt had struck the rear of the Boat near the Engine that triggered a fire. The Family tried to extinguish the fire with buckets of water, but the flames were too fast and swift. Section by section, the flames began to engulf the Boat. Diamond realized they could not put out the fast moving flames. He told the Family, "We have to abandon the boat and swim back to shore." They jumped overboard and began to swim back to shore. However, they did not notice that the Boat drifted many miles from the shore while they were trying to put out the fire. Diamond realized this when he could not see any landscape. As they swam, Diamond tried so hard to keep his Families' heads above the water, but the ocean waves were too large and powerful, and it felt as if they were on an exercise bike peddling and going nowhere. Crystal was an excellent swimmer and she took over trying to keep everyone afloat. She repeatedly went under the water, pulling them back up to the surface of the water. The Family began showing signs of exhaustion. One by one, they began to go under and drown despite Crystal's and Diamond's efforts.

Since Crystal was the best swimmer, she was the last one to go under the water. During all the excitement, she suddenly remembered that she was pregnant, but it was too late. She was exhausted and she slowly began to sink. While she was descending lower and lower under into the deep water, all of a sudden something grabbed a hold of her and then something swallowed her up.

After some time, Crystal woke up confused, dazed, and in a panic. She was inside of something because she could see through it. It looked like she was inside of a Gigantic Oyster Shell. Then all of a sudden, Crystal began to scream in pain and said, "Oh no this is not happening, it is too soon for the Baby to come!" She thought, *"How is this possible that I am still alive,*

am I dreaming this?" She began to go into labor and the Baby was born inside the Giant Oyster. It was a boy, and he was so small and premature. She was worried that the premature Baby would not survive this experience. Even though she was weak, she was a Nurse; therefore, she knew how to attend to the Baby. Crystal passed in and out of consciousness because of the low oxygen levels.

Then all of a sudden, the Giant Oyster began to move a little and began to do what Oysters do best and started to produce a smooth protected barrier around the Mother and the premature Baby. Layer upon layer the Oyster produced millions of tiny small crystals. These small crystals were formed and also somehow infused into the premature baby's body. It was almost as if the Oyster was trying to save the premature Baby's life by infusing the crystals into the Baby's body. Crystal and the premature Baby were kept alive with some oxygen stored inside of the Giant Oyster because it just so happens that there were some Mystical Mermaids nearby blowing the oxygen into the Giant Oyster shell. The Giant Oyster was translucent and glass like and Crystal could see through it. Crystal said, "Are those Mermaids? She was amazed and frightened at the same time, but she was happy that they were still alive.

As Crystal and the Baby laid inside of the Giant Oyster, she suddenly remembered something that happened to her when she was a small child. She remembered that she came from a Family of Oyster Divers and she was born on a nearby Island. She remembered on one particular day while diving for oysters with her Family; she saw something shining in the water. She moved closer to see what it was. She was amazed because it looked like a Large Oyster Clam and something swimming nearby that looked like people. Since she was a child and curious, she reached out to touch it.

All of a sudden the Oyster opened up and she got startled and swam back up to the surface of the water. Afterward, she remembered feeling a little strange. She wanted to tell her Parents, but she remembered they told her not to go near anything that was strange. So Crystal kept it a secret and out of her mind until now. Crystal wondered in her mind, *"Is this possible, could this be the same Oyster she saw about 15 years ago and how did it get so big or am I dreaming?"* Little did Crystal know, the Oyster she saw back then was no ordinary Oyster; this Oyster just so happened to be living in the Ocean right next to an undiscovered Meteor that fell to the Earth a long time ago. The Little Oyster has been feeding off small particles from the Meteorite for many years and is growing at an accelerated rate. This Oyster Clam somehow sensed and remembered the little girl from long ago and tried to protect Crystal and her premature Baby the only way it knew how and that is by forming a Pearl.

After some time went by Crystal tried to recover and to regain her strength. However, Crystal was still too weak and in still shock from what she had just witnessed. Crystal felt she was beginning to pass out again. Before she passed out, she kissed and Baby and told the Baby, "I love you" and she prayed that the Baby would survive. The Giant Oyster opened up and the Baby was taken up slowly to the surface in a protected bubble with the help of the Queen of the Mermaids. The Baby was placed on a piece of Drift Wood that was floating nearby. Some time went by and the protected Buddle soon disappeared. The Baby was alone, but remained calm and **Earl the Human Pearl** was born.

CHAPTER 2

The Rescue

HONK HONK! TOOT TOOT! It just so happens, by some slight miracle a Fishing Boat was nearby at exactly the same time the Giant Oyster opened up and released the Baby. The Crew of the Fishing boat had given up for the day because the fish were not biting. Then one of the crew of the fishing boat spotted something shining in the water and they thought their luck had changed. One of the crew members shouted, "Could it be a school of Fish!" They steered the boat closer and closer to find out what it was. Another crew member shouted, "Oh my God, it looks like a human baby, but how did it get out here!" The Crew sprang into action and jumped into the water to rescue the Baby.

After, the Crew rescued the Baby out of the water, one of the Crew members said, "Look at the Baby's skin, it is shiny and almost illuminated." They thought it was from being out in the Sun and the water for so long. They cleaned the Baby up and wrapped him in some blankets, all along wondering how the Baby survived out in the water for so long. After some time, the Baby's skin began to change to a normal tone.

Meanwhile, The Captain and Crew rushed the Baby to the Hospital to ensure his survival. After some time, the Baby was checked out, cleaned up, and monitored over night to make sure he was OK. The Captain of the Fishing Boat, who name was Ulysses Pearl, soon found out what had happened to the Baby's Family by the Coast Guard. They said, "We think the Baby is from a Family that was caught in the fast moving storm we had a week ago." Since the Baby had no Family and after a thorough search for a family member, the Captain of the Fishing Boat decided to adopt the Baby and raise the Baby as his own. The Crew gave him the name Earl Smith-La Pearl' because he was a shiny little object pulled from the Water.

As the years went by, Earl grew into a fine young Boy, however, he was haunted by strange dreams. He always dreamt of the Ocean, swimming and swimming and getting nowhere. These were always the same dreams and Earl wondered why he was having these dreams. He would always wake up sweating and drenched in water.

Earl's adoptive Father Ulysses had an idea and knew what might be wrong with Earl. He also knew it was time to tell Earl what happened to his Biological Family. Ulysses dreaded this day, but he told Earl the story. Ulysses told Earl, "You are so precious to me. I never thought I could be happy again ever since my Wife passed away. We did not have any children so when I found you it was almost like my prayers were answered. One day while the Crew and I were out fishing, we found you floating on a piece of driftwood in the middle of the Ocean. We pulled you out of the Water and took you straight to the Hospital; and that is when we found out what had happened to your biological Family. Your family all drowned at sea during a very bad Storm and by some miracle you were the only one who survived. After I found out what had happened to your family, I adopted you and raised you as my Son; and give you the Name Earl Smith-LA Pearl in honor your Biological Family." Earl cried a little, but he soon recovered because he was only a Baby at the time and he did not remember.

After the talk with his Adopted Father, Earl's bad dreams slowed down a little and he went about his life, but from time to time he would think about his Biological Family. Earl has a Birthmark on his arm that looks a little like a little Oyster Clam. He thought about someday getting it removed because the kids would tease him and call him Earl the Clam.

Over the years, Earl was taught the Fishing Business by the Captain and Crew. Earl would also get a strange feeling at the sight of Oysters. Little did Earl know, these strange tingly feelings around his Birthmark holds the key to his Destiny hiding deep within inside his body. Earl would always suppress these strange feelings because he did not understand them.

By a stroke of luck, Ulysses Fishing Business took off and he became very rich fast because no matter where they were in the Ocean the fish would gather together around the Ulysses' Fishing Boat. It was magical; the Crew was always amazed by this and thought it was because of Earl.

Later on in his life, Earl meets a young Man named Nix, who would introduce him to three more friends. Nix will tell Earl an incredible Story that will change his life forever. Earl and his other friends all became very close. They all got Jobs and worked for a worldwide computer Company called **GOBLE INTERACTIVE.**

Later on it will turn out that these five Friends has formed the ULTI-MUS MAXI-MUS crime Fighting Team and here are their life Stories.

CHAPTER 3

The Story of Nix

Nix's story also began before he was born. John and Emerald Hawks were Zoologists and rescuers of Animals. One day while out on location, John and Emerald were looking for new animals to save. They saw a strange light at a distance so they moved closer to find out what it was. As they moved closer and closer to the light, it began to shine brighter and brighter.

They then came across a cliff, so they climbed up. As they looked down, they saw something that looked like a Bird inside of a Ring of Fire. John asked, "What is it?" Emerald whispered, "This is amazing, could this be what I think it is?" John answered, "Yes, I think it is the Mythical Phoenix Bird. This is a once in a lifetime event and it looks like we are in the middle of this event."

As John and Emerald observed from the top of the cliff, parts of the cliff gave way and Emerald slipped and fell down into the Ring of Fire. John shouted, "This is not good!" because Emerald was pregnant. John tried to climb down the cliff to aid his Wife, but somehow he was frozen in place; however, he could still see what was happening. So he prayed that his Wife and Unborn child would be OK. Emerald screamed in pain and she began to go into labor, and there was nothing John could do. The fire began to consume the Bird and Emerald. The Baby was born at the exact same time as the Phoenix Bird made the change and was resurrected from the ashes.

Emerald survived, but not without some burns on her body, and the Baby was unharmed. Then all of a sudden, John was unfrozen and he was able to climb down the cliff to aid his Wife and newborn Baby. Even though they were still in shock, they looked over to observe the newborn Phoenix Bird. The new Phoenix Bird froze them in place again and communicated with them without speaking. The Phoenix told them, "You are right, I am the Phoenix of ancient times. John, I could not let you in because you would not have survived. I could only protect one from the flames. So I chose your Wife and child. The Baby received most of the protection. Your wife received partial protection." The Phoenix blew on Emerald and she was healed from her burns.

The Phoenix Bird then told them, "You and your Baby have been given a gift. Do not reveal what you have just witnessed because only a few have witnessed this event. In addition, Emerald, you have a twin Sister. You were separated at Birth. So seek her out before it is too late. Also, your Baby is safe, but as he grows older, he will possess very special powers."

"We understand and thank you," said John and Emerald. Then they fell into a deep sleep and found themselves back in their house. They named their newborn Baby Nix because of his unusual Birth that was connected to the Phoenix Bird. They also started the search to find Emerald's Twin Sister and their search turned up nothing, but they never gave up. The premature Baby grew in strength and everything seemed normal. From time to time, Emerald and John thought of that day, but always remembered what the Phoenix Bird told them and they never revealed to anyone what happened on the Day when their Baby was born. One day while playing with the Baby, the parents noticed that the Baby has the ability to communicate with them without talking. This was the same way the Phoenix communicated with them. They were amazed, but did not reveal this to anyone because they knew that no one would believe them. Every day they discovered something different about Baby Nix's abilities.

One day while out playing in the yard, Nix came to close to the barbecue grill. And John tried to stop him, but it was too late. Some of the charcoal fell on him, but he was not burned. They looked at each other and they were amazed. On another day while Emerald was cleaning the house,

Nix was left alone and he wandered into a room with an open window. Just like a toddler, he was curious and climbed out of the window onto a ledge. Emerald soon discovered what happened and tried to get the Baby off of the ledge. Baby Nix slipped and fell off of the ledge. Amazingly, he was able to stop himself in midair. He steadied himself and ascended back in the window. Emerald told John what happened, but they still did not reveal Nix's powers.

Nix's Parents had a small animal Sanctuary and Nix loved to play with the animals. So one day while out playing with the animals, the parents noticed another one of his abilities. He had the ability to change into any animal that he touched. Nix's abilities were becoming unlimited. They knew his abilities were somehow connected to his unusual Birth. Baby Nix grew into a young boy, and then into a young Man. Nix was slow to age and he looked younger than he was. To hide his healing abilities, Nix enrolled into a Medical Program because it was not time for him to reveal himself. Nix was also haunted by a little voice whispering to him, "Do not reveal yourself yet, you must find Earl, you must find Earl."

The years went on and the Family moved to New York when Nix was still a young Man because they had a lead on their search for Emerald's Sister. From time to time, the little voice would whisper to Nix, "You must find Earl." So Nix sought out on his quest to find this person named Earl.

CHAPTER 4

The Story of Merlo

Merlo had an ordinary upbringing. Merlo father Plutock was a famous Magician that comes from a long line of Magicians. Merlo Father has the Houdini like ability to escape from any bounds. However, these were only magic tricks. On this one particular day, Merlo Father allowed him to assist him with his Magical act on stage. Merlo was so excited and he was a natural. He performed as if he did magic all his life. They performed all the traditional magic tricks along with the famous Disappearing Act. The crowd went wild and gave them a standing ovation. The Act went flawlessly.

After the Act, they met a Man who said, "I loved your show and I would like to have a word with you if I may? My Name is Namojchee Lee and I am a Biochemist; I work for a Chemical firm. I have made a discovery that my company does not know about. Don't worry, this discovery was created by me and in my Home. I have been watching you and your Son for a long time and I have chosen you for something special because I believe you would keep and make good of my discovery."

Mr. Namojchee further explained, "I stumbled on my discovery quite by accident. I was experimenting with some chemicals that would enable solid mass objects to appear lighter. While I was working, a small rock dropped into the Vial of chemicals. I became startled and reached into the Vial to pull it out, but without my protected gloves. I pulled my hand out right away and rushed to wash off the chemicals. While on my way to the sink, my hand started to change colors, then completely disappeared before my eyes. I got nervous and washed it off with some distilled water and my hand started to appear again, but not completely. So I washed my hand off some more and it reappeared. As I said before, I am a Biochemist so I conducted more experiments on the substance. And I found out later that it was the rock that fell into the Vial of chemicals. It turned out that the small rock was a small meteorite from the Planet Pluto. The Planet Pluto was named after the God of Invisibility."

Mr. Namojchee pulled out a container and some sort of head gear and asked Merlo Father to put the substance on his son's arm to start. "Don't worry, it will not harm the Boy." Plutock was a little skeptical at first, but he went on with Namojchee's request. Within moments the boy's arm became invisible. Namojchee rubbed another substance on the boy's arm and his arm became visible again. Namojchee said, "I know you have questions, but I have been watching you for a while. I chose you and not my Company or the Military because I think you will make good of my discovery and use it for good and not exploit it for greed and power. I was a very sick man because of the some of the chemicals that I have been working with, but not anymore."

Merlo and his Father soon discovered that not only does the Chemical Substance render you invisible, but the user has great speed and agility. Mr. Namojchee told Merlo and his Father, "No one would question you and your son because you are Magicians. They would assume it is magic tricks. It would be the perfect cover because everyone knows that Magicians do not reveal their secrets."

Over the next year, Mr. Namojchee showed Merlo and his Father the Ins' and Outs' of his discovery and how to master it. He told them that the secret to turning on and off the illusion of invisibility is in this Helmet that he created. Mr. Namojchee said, "Please use this wisely."

Merlo and his Father continued with their Magic shows, but the Grand Finale of the Disappearing Man was better than ever. They began to travel the World and became rich and famous, but not without some attention from the Military. Just like Mr. Namojchee said the Military assumes it was just Magic tricks and knew they would not get any secrets.

CHAPTER 5

The Story of Malia and Celia

Malia and Celia Lee amazing story begins when they were children. They were raised by their Father Mr. Namojchee Lee after their Mother passed away. Mr. Namojchee is a Genius who works as a Biochemist. Their Mother was American and their father was born in the Asia Pacific who came to America when he was a Child.

One day the Girls were home with the Babysitter because the Father was out on a Job assignment. He was in a hurry and running late, so he left his Laboratory door open. The Girls wandered into their Fathers Lab because they were always curious about their Father's work. They looked around at the colorful Chemicals with amazement. Celia said, "Look at this, it smell so good and it is so pretty." Malia told Celia to "put that down" and Celia said, "No." They began to wrestle and Celia drops the Vial of chemicals. It spilled all over the floor. Celia said, "Look at what you made me do. Father will be so upset." Malia said, "We need to clean up this mess before the babysitter finds us and before Father gets back." As they were cleaning up the chemicals off of the floor, Malia said, "I don't feel so good Celia." And Celia said, "I feel funny too." They rushed to the bathroom and began to vomit. Later that day they felt a little better, but they did not tell the babysitter and their Father what they had done.

One particular day while playing in the yard, they Girls noticed this strange glow that began to surround their bodies. Malia asked Celia, "What is happening to us?" They got scared and told their Father. Their Father said, "What substance did you mess with?" They said, "It was the pretty Blue liquid." Namojchee realized it was the Mace Pepper Spray that he was working on for the Military. He was trying to make the spray more potent, but not harmful to the recipient of the spray. Mr. Namojchee wondered, *"How were they able to absorb the substance without being harmed."* He thought, *"Maybe because he was using the Herbs called Mace."* Mr.

Namojchee tried to counter the affect with a neutralizing chemical. It worked and the Girls got better.

One day Mr. Namojchee noticed the Girls playing in the yard with their Dogs and there was some kind of a Mist that was coming from their bodies. When they touched the dogs, the dogs shivered and fell down. He called out to the Girls and said, "Girls, what did you do to the Dogs?" They said, "Nothing Father, we were playing with the Dogs and they fell down." The Dogs were not dead, but they were knocked out for a while. Mr. Namojchee soon discovered the effects of the Mace chemical on his Girls. They had the ability to render the animals unconscious. Mr. Namojchee thought to himself, *"If this worked on animals then what about people?"* So like any Scientist he asked the Girls to touch him on the arm and nothing happened. He thought, *"That was strange."* So he was on a quest to find out what was triggering their ability. Namojchee soon discovered it was triggered when the Girls got excited about something. So Mr. Namojchee taught the Girls how to control their emotions and harness their powers.

Time went on and Mr. Namojchee met Merlo and his father at a Magic show. Before that Mr. Namojchee ran across Nix when he was in a car accident. Mr. Namojchee Lee was badly hurt and unconscious. Nix saw the accident and came to Mr. Namojchee's aid. He placed his hands on Mr. Namojchee and fell into a trance and Mr. Namojchee was instantly healed along with his chemical induce sickness. Mr. Namojchee was amazed at what had just happened. He said, "I feel great." And then he asked Nix, "What did you do to me?" Nix answered and said without talking, *"My name is Nix and I have read your thoughts and memories."* Mr. Namojchee said, "Oh, you did, but how?"

Nix told Mr. Namojchee his amazing story. After that Mr. Namojchee introduced Nix to his Twin Girls, Malia and Celia and then to Merlo and his Father.

CHAPTER 6

The Quest to Find Earl

Nix told Mr. Namojchee, Merlo, Malia and Celia about his Quest to find someone named Earl. Nix told the others, "From time to time, I hear a voice whispering to me, you must find Earl before it is too late and you will know him when you find him. I have been looking for him for a while now and I know I am getting really close because the whispering voice told me so. It turns out that he is my Cousin. His Mother and my Mother were Twins that were separated at Birth and we have been looking for him ever since the Phoenix revealed this. Earl does not know this, but I plan to tell him. So, I need your help to speed up my Quest." So Nix and the others started out on their mission to find Earl, but a lot of cues led to nothing.

On one particular day, Nix homed in on Man because he heard the Man call out the name Earl and Nix had a strange feeling. Earl and his Adoptive Father Ulysses were on a Safari Adventure vacation at a Theme Park. Earl somehow got separated from his Adoptive Father and became a little disoriented because the Theme Park was huge. Earl heard something calling him; he came across something that looked like a Bird and a Man. The Bird-like creature communicated to him without talking. The Bird Creature said, "Hello Earl my Name is Nicolas, but you can call me Nix for short." "I have been looking for you for a very long time," Earl replied. "Earl, you are holding back something within you and I understand because I like you possess a secret within. I am what some May call a Shifter and this is not my real form," Nix said as he changed back into a young Man.

Earl was startled at first, but he still listened to the Young Man. Nix continued and told Earl, "Do not to be afraid. We are related through our Mothers who were Twin Girls that were separated at Birth." Earl asked Nix, "How did you come to know this?" Nix said, "I often hear a voice whispering to me telling me you must find Earl before it is too late. This little voice who I think is the mystical Phoenix Bird, who saved my life when I was born and who is communicating these things to me. The voice told me to seek you out before it is too late and to tell you the true story of why you were found drifting on a piece of driftwood when you were just a Baby. The voice said you will know him when you find him."

Earl replied, "A little bird told you this?" Nix replied, "No, it was the

Mystical Phoenix Bird, who I said saved my life when I was born." Nix saw that Earl was becoming skeptical. So Nix told Earl the whole story of what happened to him when he was born and how the Phoenix Bird saved his life and told his parents not to reveal it and they never did.

Earl said, "My Adoptive Father told me the story of how he found me drifting on a piece of Driftwood and told me how he thought I was destined to be his son, but he never told me any more than that." Nix said, "Your Adoptive Father did not know this part of the story." Nix told Earl everything the Phoenix Bird revealed to him. Nix said, "As I told you before, when I was born in the in the nest of the Phoenix Bird, the Phoenix froze my parents in time and peaked into their minds and saw their memories. That is when the Phoenix Bird learned about your Mother and my Mother being Twin Sisters." Earl accepted the story because he and Nix have a strange resemblance to each other. **Nix told Earl to. "Buckle your seat belt and hold on tight because I am going to tell you the true nature of your Birthmark in the shape of an Oyster Clam."** Nix asked Earl, "Do you remember when you tried to learn how to swim and you kept sinking to the bottom like something was pulling at you? Well, it was the something pulling at you and trying to communicate with you."

Nix further revealed to Earl what he is eventually to become. Nix touches Earl on the arm that had the Birthmark and threw some water in his face. Earl's Birthmark grew and something began to cover his entire body. Earl became startled and began to panic. Earl asked, "What is this?" Then Earl shouted, "Get this off of me! Get it off of me!" Nix told Earl, "Calm down Earl and do not panic because it is the essence of the Giant Oyster that kept you alive when you were just a premature Baby who was born inside of a Giant Oyster." Earl replied, "That is impossible. How can anybody be inside of an Oyster?" Nix said, "Stay with me Earl. You know the story of what happen to your Biological Family?" Earl said, "Yes, they all drowned in a bad storm." Nix replied, "Well that part is true, but during that time, your Mother was Pregnant with you and she was the last to go under after trying to save your Family. As she was descending under the water, she was grabbed by some Mermaids and placed inside of the Giant Oyster. While inside of the Oyster, you were born. You and your Mother was kept alive with the help of the Mermaids who provided the Oxygen. As you know Oysters secretes a thin layer of calcium carbonate like substance which forms a pearl when it thinks it is an intruder. So, the Giant Oyster infused your premature Body with millions of small tiny crystals. This was done to save your life. Layer upon layer the Oyster did the work." Earl asked, "Are you telling me I was born inside of a Giant Oyster?" "This was no ordinary Oyster. This Oyster just so happened to be living in the Ocean right next to an undiscovered Meteor from the Planet Saturn that fell to the Earth many years ago. The little Oyster fed off small Meteorite particles and grew at an enormous rate," Nix replied.

Earl looked amazed and frightened at the same time. Earl started to get nervous, but then he suddenly remembered his strange Birthmark that tingled from time to time. Nix told Earl, "I know this sounds strange, but stay with me. Your Biological Mother Crystal encountered this Oyster when she was just a small child, but she put it out of her mind until she was inside of the Giant Oyster. Your Mother was weak and she did not survive. Your Mother prayed that you would survive and you did. The Giant Oyster opened up and you were taken up to the surface with the help of the Mermaids and were placed on a piece of driftwood. That is when your Adoptive father Ulysses found you and save your life." Nix continued to tell Earl, "I am glad you did not remove your Birthmark because it would have killed you and you would have triggered the essence of the Pearl deep with inside you. You would have not been ready for that experience. I know you always wondered how your Mother looked. Here is a picture of my Mother and that should answer your question." Earl stared at the picture for a very long time. Earl could not help noticing the resemblance between himself and Nix.

Nix also showed Earl some of his other Forms. ***Nix told Earl to, "Buckle up again, I would like to show you that you that we are not alone."*** Nix clapped his hands together and all of a sudden three other figures appeared. Earl became startled again. One was dressed in all white and appeared almost illuminated. The other two were two girls who looked like they were Twins. Nix told Earl, "This is Merlo (Code Named **Merlock**) and the girls are Malia and Celia (Code Names the **"Maci Twins"**) and as you know I am Nix (Code Name **"Phoenix"**) and you are Earl (Code name **"THE PEARL"**) because of your unusual Birth inside of the Giant Oyster.

Nix told Earl, "Even though we all have our special abilities that is powerful and unique. Our powers can be an unstoppable force when combined together and you Earl are the missing Key. All of this was revealed to me by the Phoenix Bird." The Phoenix said, "It is in Earl's voice vibrations that are known as Chakras. According to Hindu Buddhist belief, Chakras are pools of energy that are confined in our bodies and yours is a special Voice Chakra. So, Earl whenever you are in any situations that you cannot get out of by yourself, just say these words 'ULTI-MUS MAXI-MUS CHANGE TO THE PEARL' and it will start a change reaction that will transform each of us into an unstoppable force."

Earl was happy to finally have some friends his age because most of the time it was him, his Father and the Fishing Crew. Earl and the others became lifelong Friends and always protected each other without using their special abilities. They all learned the Marital Arts and became Masters of the Arts. Nix taught Earl to control and harness his power, just like he taught the others. Nix told the team, "We all have been given gifts, and we need to make a promise to only use our power for good and only as a last resort."

CHAPTER 7
Ultimus Maximus versus the Tasers

The power of the Team is revealed on one very Stormy Day. Earl and his Friends were working out at one of their friend's Gym. They were in their exercise routines and having fun. A Gang of guys came into the Gym and started to tease Earl, Nix, Merlo and especially the Twin Girls. They said, "What do we have here?" Another said, "It looks like a bunch of Nerds trying to get in shape." Earl did not like to be teased because it reminded him of when he was teased when he was a boy. *Earl the Clam, Earl the Clam*, ran though his mind. Earl asked them to "STOP IT" and they did not. Earl confronted the Leader of the Gang and then more of the Gang Members showed up. Earl and his Friends knew they were outnumbered, so they backed out and left because they did not want any trouble at their friend's Gym.

After that Earl and his Friends wanted to get something to eat. They eventually found themselves a Restaurant and had some lunch. They were eating, having fun, and playing Video Games. All of a sudden, the same group of guys showed up. They were looking around and acting very suspicious. One of the Gang members pulled out a Taser Weapons and told the Cashier to, "Hand over all your money." The Cashier refused and the

Leader slapped her across the face with the Taser Gun and she fell to the floor. People began to panic and started to run. The Gang started shooting into the crowd of people and everyone scattered. Earl started to get very angry after he saw what the Gang was doing. They were tasing and shooting so many people. Earl said, "I think I know who these guys are. They are the infamous Tasers Gang that I heard about on Television. They use jacked up high powered Tasers to render their victims unconscious, then rob their victims of their processions."

The Leader spotted Earl and his Friends and said, "Look, it is those guys again." Then they directed their attention to Earl and his Friends and began to fire on them. Earl and his Friends slipped behind some tables. Earl's mild manner began to change to anger and began to be uncontrollable. Earl looked at Nix and the rest of his Friends. They nodded, as if all was in agreement about something.

With all in agreement, Earl clapped his hand once and it made the sound of Thunder Clouds. Earl started to chant the words, "'ULTIMUS MAXIMUS CHANGE TO THE PEARL'." Earl began shifting into The Ulti-mus Maxi-mus Pearl with weapons loaded. Earl's body turned into a shiny hard substance that is virtually impenetrable to anything known to man. This power comes from the combination of the Rock Hard Meteorite and Rock Hard Pearl Shell hidden deep within side Earl's body.

When Earl chanted these words it also triggers his SIDE-KICKS into action. The Phoenix ULTIMUS, who is the most powerful and the Master Mind that brought the Team together to form the ULTI-MUS MAXI-MUS. Merlo is a Maximus Magician, no doors or locks can hold or bound him. The Macy Twins Maximus holds a venomous like substance 10 times more effective as Mace and renders anything Human or Animal unconscious with only a touch.

Meanwhile, the Tasers Gang was startled by what they just witnessed and ran outside. While outside, the Tasers' Leader signal to his four men called the '4 CORNERS' to surround Earl and attack him from all four sides. They began shooting at the Ultimus Maximus Team again. The bullets bounced off of The PEARL'S Rock Hard body and ricocheted everywhere. The Pearl and his Sidekicks began their assault. They charged into the Tasers like they were toys. Bodies were flying everywhere. Merlo went through the Gang with lightning speed and tying them up as he went along. The Maci Twins showered them with their Mace like substance rendering them helpless to resist. The Phoenix froze some of them in place.

The rest of Gang Members saw what was happening, then retreated and ran away because this was one fight they did not expect.

The Police arrived on the scene and caught some of the Gang Members and arrested them. One of the Gang Members was rambling on about thunder and People changing into other People. By now, Earl and his Sidekicks returned back into their normal forms. However, before the Police could question them, Earl and his Friends left the crime scene. The Police found some little round stones at the crime scene and sent them out to be analyzed. It was all on the CBN News and in the Newspapers. The News announcer stated, "There seems to be some kind of vigilantes group out there who beat up a group that had long been known as the Tasers. We don't know who they are right now, but the Police are on the watch for them because they still have a lot of questions for them."

Meanwhile, the rest of the Gang Members met back at their hideout. The Leader said, "Did you see that?" "Yeah who was those Guys!" another shouted. The Gang's Leader said angrily, "I don't know, but I am going to find out!" After the battle, the robbers were on a quest to find out who those guys were. They asked questions around the area neighborhoods, but their quest turned up nothing that they could use. Earl and his Friends got wind of the Gang Members asking questions around the area neighborhoods so Earl and his Friends were also on the watch.

CHAPTER 8

The Maci Twins are Kidnapped

One day Malia and Celia went out on a date with some Guys they met. They thought they were just going out for dinner and to have some fun, but little did they know, their new found Friends had other intentions. One of the guys said, "I have to make a stop." And he went into a store. Malia said, "This place seems familiar to me." She became nervous, because she began to recognize the store. Malia said, "This is the place that some are suspected of kidnapping girls, but the police could not prove it because they kept findings nothing, but a Storefront. Malia knew these facts because she has Friends in the Police Department. Malia got nervous and called Earl, but she was cut short because one of the guys ran out of the Store after he saw Malia talking on her Cell phone. He told her to "hang up the phone." Malia said angrily, "Excuse me who do you think you are talking to like that!" All of a sudden a Girl ran out of the store and told the Girls to "run." A man grabbed the girl and took her back in the Store.

Malia and Celia tried to fight them off and run, but the Men caught up with them and threw them back into the car. Celia was hit over the head, so she did not get a chance to trigger her Powers. Malia managed to fight them off before she could get hit. She managed to open the car door and jumped out on to the street, but not before she was shot in the arm with some kind of sleep agent and tracking Gun. Malia knows she was helpless to trigger her power because she and her sister would have to be together for it to happen. Malia knew Celia would be alright because the guys did not know who she was and what she was capable of. Malia kept running and came across a Police Station, but she began to hallucinate and thought the Policeman was the Kidnappers. She thought the Police said I told you there was no where you could run. So she kept running, but she was beginning to feel the effects of the sleep agent. She called Earl again, but the effect of the Sleep Gun began to take its toll. She was just was rambling on so Earl could not understand what she was saying. She passed out and eventually and she was caught again by the Kidnappers.

Meanwhile, Earl was trying to piece together what Malia was trying to tell him. He began the chant, "'ULTI-MUS MAX-IMUS CHANGE TO THE PEARL, CHANGE TO THE PEARL'." This time only Merlo and Phoenix showed up. He told them about Malia Cell phone call. He told the Phoenix, "I need you to home into Celia and Malia's thoughts." Earl said to the Phoenix, "I know I told you never to read our thoughts, but this might be a matter of life and death." The Phoenix closed his eyes and opened them up again. His eyes were as red as fire, then he went into a trance, and homed in on Malia and Celia's thoughts. He made contact and told Earl and Merlo, "They were alive, but they seemed weak as if they were semi-conscious or something." The Phoenix said, "I think they may have been drugged or something, but I know where they are."

They found the location that looked like a warehouse where the Guys were holding Malia and Celia. Earl said, "Not these Guys again." **It was the Tasers Gang again**. The Girls were tied up and it look like The Tasers were trying to brainwash them.

The Pearl, Merlo, and Phoenix dropped down into the room like they were descending Birds and landed on the floor of the warehouse. The Pearl told Merlo to, "Unlock the girl's bounds and free them up." The Tasers pulled out their weapons and fired. The bullets bounced off of The Pearl's body and right back at the Tasers Gang. The Pearl said, "I see these guys have not learned." The Pearl and Phoenix charged through the Tasers and bodies were flying everywhere because the Gang was not very good shooters.

The Pearl told Phoenix to, "Go help Merlock, free the Girls and I will handle these Guys." Merlock managed to free the girls, but they were out of it. The Phoenix has the power of healing and he began his healing Magic. The Phoenix eyes began to glow red again and he pulled the girls out of their medicated state. To pull Malia and Celia into the Group, Earl had to begin the chant again "'ULTI-MUS MAXI-MUS CHANGE TO THE PEARL'." Malia and Celia started their change and they were all on board. The Tasers saw what was happening and ran away because they knew what was going to happen next. As before, this was one fight they knew they could not win. The Team all rejoiced and hugged each other to celebrate their Victory. Earl said, "Why do these guys keep starting these fights and run away."

Meanwhile back at the Tasers second hideout, the Tasers' Leader said, "This is the second time we ran into these guys so we got to find out what these guys weaknesses are." The Tasers' Leader mentioned, "Have you noticed the one guy chants some words and then they all began to change into something else?" The Tasers Gang's Leader said, "Somehow we have to get this guy alone and shut up his mouth."

Later on television that night the News announcer reported, "It looks like the Vigilantes struck again. This time some guys were found beat up and tied up in a warehouse. There were no sign of our helpful vigilantes."

CHAPTER 9

Earl is Ambushed in Korea

For a time, things started to return back to normal. Meanwhile, Earl had to fly to South Korea on a work assignment. While out on his work assignment in Korea, Earl noticed that something did not seem quite right. He noticed some People in the crowd was eyeing him and they did not look Korean. Earl got spooked and hid behind a building. He thought he recognized some of the people as being part of the Tasers Gang. He thought to himself, *"I must be seeing things...is this possible?"* However, before Earl could gather his thoughts someone jumped him from behind and grabbed his hand. Earl was startled and began to wrestle with the person. Earl asked the guy, "What is your problem Man?" Earl's steered at the guy and recognized him as being one the Tasers Gang Members. Then out of nowhere more of the Tasers showed up and they tried to tie up Earl's Mouth because this was their only chance to get him.

Earl got free and begun the Chant, "'ULTI-MUS MAXI-MUS CHANGE TO THE PEARL', 'CHANGE TO THE PEARL'." Earl's four Sidekicks showed up and the Tasers ran away. Earl shouted, "These Guys are really beginning to piss me off!"

Later that day while Earl was relaxing in his Hotel room, there was a knock at the door. Earl opened the door and to his surprise, it was the Tasers Gang again. The Leader shouted, "Hey Big Mouth!" And then he tried to tie up Earl's Mouth so he would not trigger his Sidekicks. He pushed Earl and Earl pushed him back and the Leader slid behind a wall. Earl thought, *"That was interesting."* More of the Tasers showed up and they also tried to tie up Earl's mouth. Earl escaped their clutches with a few Martial Art maneuvers and with the help of an assault weapon. The Tasers' Leader began to notice that The Pearl was fighting alone and without the others. The Leader asked Earl, "Why didn't you call the others?" The Pearl replied, "Surprise I don't need to call them all of the time and that is only for special effects."

Meanwhile, Earl was running out of bullets because there were so many of them. He managed to find some more bullets in his pocket. Earl said, "I have to make these shots count!" and he did. Earl shot the Gang's Leader and he went down, but this tough cookie began to move again. With no bullets left, Earl found one of the Taser guns. Earl could have just finished the Leader off with just his brute strength, but he decided to give the Leader a taste of his own medicine. He Tased the Leader and he was out. Later that day, Earl summoned the others and told them what happened. Nix told Earl, "We have to be on the watch for others out there because I think these guys don't give up easy."

EARL AND THE TEAM FINALLY DEFEATED THE LOW LEVEL CRIMINALS CALLED THE TASERS GANG AND THE ADVENTURES WILL CONTINUE WITH NEW CHARACTERS

Book 2:

The Adventures of Earl the Human Pearl and Friends
And the Search for Earl's Mother

Earl's Mother might still be alive. She was absorbed by the Giant Oyster who has been keeping her alive. Crystal's body is incased inside of a Giant Pearl. Nix thought it was the Phoenix Bird whispering to him, but it will turn out that it was Earl Mother who told him the Story of Earl's astonishing Birth inside of the Oyster Shell. She will be rescued and she will be bringing along some Friends.

Also, when Earl Tased the Leader of the Tasers Gang he was still in Pearl form and that was a big mistake. It turned out that some of the essence of Pearl went through the Taser Gun. Earl missed the Leader's heart and the Taser gun sent an electrical charge though his body. The Leader was later found by one of the Gang Members. The Ultimus Maximus Team will really be tested when The Tasers regroup and form another more powerful Gang called the **STINGERS**.

ABOUT THE AUTHOR

J. Allen is a retired Military members of the Air Forces. She always enjoyed watching good Science Fiction and Adventures Story no matter how old she is. She is an author who thought up the Story of Earl while going through some old writings. It started out with just piecing some things together and coming up with a little Story that became a bigger Story. Her Co-workers encouraged her to come up with more to the Story. So the Little Story of Earl became a bigger Story of Earl and eventually turned into The Adventures of Earl the Human Pearl and Friends.

www.ingramcontent.com/pod-product-compliance
Lightning Source LLC
Chambersburg PA
CBHW061814290426
44110CB00026B/2873